For Gabrielle—D.F.

For my best friend, Amanda!—J.H.

Scholastic Australia
An imprint of Scholastic Australia Pty Limited
PO Box 579 Gosford NSW 2250
ABN 11 000 614 577
www.scholastic.com.au

Part of the Scholastic Group
Sydney • Auckland • New York • Toronto • London • Mexico City • New Delhi • Hong Kong • Buenos Aires • Puerto Rico

First published by Scholastic Australia in 2021.
This edition published in 2022.

A catalogue record for this book is available from the National Library of Australia

ISBN: 9781761124914

Typeset in Argone LC and Flapstick.

Printed in China by RR Donnelley.

Scholastic Australia's policy, in association with RR Donnelley, is to use papers that are renewable and made efficiently from wood grown in responsibly managed forests, so as to minimise its environmental footprint.

10 9 8 7 6 5 4 3 2 24 25 26 / 2

How to MAKE a FRIEND in 6 Easy STEPS

DHANA FOX

JAMES HART

A Scholastic Australia Book

Rosie wanted a friend.

Apparently, making friends was easy.
It said so in Rosie's new book.
Rosie stayed up late reading.

FISH
PUFFS

The next morning, Rosie gulped down her breakfast and swam to the shipwreck.

Rosie was **ready** to make a friend.

Step One:
Smile.

'Argh!'

Step Two:
Introduce Yourself with a Fun Fact.

'My name's Rosie. I have fifty-two teeth.'

'Yikes!'

Step Three:
Say Something Nice.

'What glorious, glittering scales
you all have. Perfect for spotting
in the deep, dark sea.'
'Swim for your life!'

Step Four:
Entertain with a Party Trick.

'Jeepers!'

Step Five:
Share Your Favourite Game or Hobby.

'I love playing hide and seek.
I sniff. I sneak. I shriek . . .
boo!'

'HELP!'

There was one final step.

Rosie was so excited.

She was about to make her very first friend!

Step Six:
Ask Your New Friend to Play.

'Would you like to play with me?'

'Hello? Hellooo?'
Where did everyone go?
Rosie wondered.

There was no new friend for Rosie.

She was all **alone**.

Until . . .

'Oof!'

'Hi. My name's Mini. I'm an **apex predator**.

You're as **cute** as a button. I could **gobble** you up.

I can do the best **bomb dives**.

I love making **sushi**.

Would you like to **play** with me?'

Rosie couldn't believe it.

This gigantic creature wanted to . . .
play?

Brilliant!

'Hi. My name's Rosie. I have fifty-two teeth.
Don't you look dapper in your black and white suit!'

SCHOOL BOOK LABELS

Just peel off and stick on!

Name:

Class:

Subject: